WASHINGTON, D.C.

A PICTORIAL SOUVENIR

CAROL M. HIGHSMITH AND TED LANDPHAIR

WASHINGTON, D.C.

A PICTORIAL SOUVENIR

CRESCENT BOOKS

NEW YORK

THE AUTHORS GRATEFULLY ACKNOWLEDGE
THE SERVICES, ACCOMMODATIONS, AND SUPPORT PROVIDED BY
HILTON HOTELS CORPORATION
IN CONNECTION WITH THE COMPLETION OF THIS BOOK.

———————

This 1997 edition is published by Crescent Books,
a division of Random House Value Publishing, Inc.,
201 East 50th Street, New York, NY 10022.

Crescent Books and colophon are trademarks of
Random House Value Publishing, Inc.

Random House
New York • Toronto • London • Sydney • Auckland
http://www.randomhouse.com/

Printed and bound in China

Library of Congress Cataloging-in-Publication Data
Highsmith, Carol M., 1946–
Washington, D.C. / Carol M. Highsmith and Ted Landphair.
p.   cm. — (A pictorial souvenir)
ISBN 0-517-20142-9
1. Washington (D.C.) — Pictorial works. I. Landphair, Ted. 1942–
II. Title. III. Series: Highsmith, Carol M., 1946–   Pictorial souvenir.
F195.H52 1997   97-11303
975.3—dc21   CIP

8   7   6   5   4   3   2   1

———————

Designed by Robert L. Wiser, Archetype Press, Inc., Washington, D.C.

PAGES 2–3: The White House, Washington Monument, and Jefferson Memorial present a stirring tableau at dusk. Once a miasmal bog and a tangle of bramble bushes, the lush ceremonial core of Washington today draws visitors from around the world.

FOREWORD

Our capital city, Washington, D.C., has been called "America's last company town," "democracy's home town," and "home office of the nation." Carved out, at the close of the eighteenth century, of some of the thickest woods and foulest swamps north of Georgia, Washington, the last alabaster city still gleaming, is amongst America's most stately, most beautiful, and most impressive. Indeed, once maligned by Charles Dickens as simply "spacious avenues that begin in nothing and lead nowhere; streets a mile long that only want houses, roads, and inhabitants; public buildings that need but a public to be complete," Washington, D.C., at the end of the twentieth century, is a powerful symbol of not only our nation but of democracy.

George Washington personally commissioned Major Pierre-Charles L'Enfant, an inveterate dreamer, to design the Federal City in 1792. L'Enfant's sketches laid out a logical grid, interrupted by wide boulevards, squares, and circles, and slashing radials reminiscent of his native Paris, and what he called a "vast esplanade," which we now know as the Washington Mall, inspired by Versailles. "The Plan of the City of Washington" converted murky Tiber Creek into a spendid canal up which the romantic architect envisioned each new president floating to his inauguration.

Long famous as an oddly dozy metropolis, as recently as 1961 John F. Kennedy could still wryly observe that it was a city of "southern efficiency and northern charm." But, by the 1990s, Washington had mushroomed into a region of four and one half million people. Today, spanning the Potomac in majestic fashion, the city fans out gracefully, offering a multitude of pleasures to the more than twenty million tourists who visit annually. Official Washington, of course, is a staggering array of historic landmarks. The imposing Lincoln and Jefferson Memorials, completed in 1922 and 1943, respectively; the White House, residence of every American president since John Adams; the Capitol, home to the Senate and House of Representatives; the Supreme Court Building, a marble temple dedicated to the law; the soaring obelisk of the Washington Monument; the Mall itself—all these are vivid reminders of the past and present of our nation.

Cultural and tourist sites abound in Washington, as well. The Smithsonian Institution is comprised of an eclectic and enlightening mix of art, history, and science museums, most of which are found on Independence Avenue and the Mall. First chartered by Congress in 1818, the Smithsonian is now one of the most illustrious institutions in the world. Indeed, the most visited museum across the globe, according to the Smithsonian, is its Air and Space Museum, which opened in 1976. Its twenty-three galleries display rare aircraft—including the Wright Brothers' 1903 flyer and Charles Lindbergh's famous plane. From the Library of Congress to the National Portrait Gallery; from Arlington National Cemetery to the Capitol's reflecting pool; the National Cathedral to the Museum of Natural History's fabled elephant to tranquil Pershing Park; the charm of its celebrated Cherry Blossom Festival to the somber beauty of the Vietnam Wall; from bustling Market Square to the profoundly moving Holocaust Museum— Washington, D.C., a city of lush public gardens and parks, is also a city of inspiring dignity.

Proud, impressive, with a grandeur and a glory befitting the capital meant to rival those of ancient Greece or Rome—Washington, D.C. belongs to all of those who prize democracy.

OVERLEAF: Because Congress has held sway over the City of Washington, no high-rise buildings, save for the Washington Monument, were permitted to obscure the grandeur. So the city spread out rather than up. Where gargantuan government buildings now stretch toward the horizon, factories, churches, rooming houses, and even a rowdy neighborhood called "Murder Row" once stood. A fetid canal ran along what is now Constitution Avenue, railroad tracks and freight yards once cluttered the Mall, and squalid row houses reached almost to the Capitol.

ABOVE: Daniel Chester French designed the nineteen-foot-tall statue that is the centerpiece of the memorial to Abraham Lincoln.

Congress had incorporated a Lincoln Monument Association in 1867, but construction did not begin until 1914. President Lincoln's only surviving son,

Robert Todd Lincoln, was in attendance when the memorial, designed by architect Henry Bacon, was dedicated on May 30, 1922. OPPOSITE: Like a lighthouse, the

Washington Monument serves as a familiar beacon, visible from many corners of the city. It and other national landmarks, including the Lincoln

Memorial and U.S. Capitol, inspire poets, brighten the nighttime sky, and provide a memorable view for passengers descending into National Airport.

Architect Robert Mills's design for the Washington Monument called for a soaring obelisk and a circular, colonnaded "pantheon of heroes." General Washington was to be depicted riding a chariot. But when construction resumed in 1876 after a hiatus of many years, engineer Thomas Casey simplified the design and eliminated the pantheon. OPPOSITE: Because the Jefferson Memorial on the Potomac River Tidal Basin stands apart from other monuments, it draws fewer visitors than the Lincoln Memorial upriver.

When the cherry blossoms bloom in early spring, visitors and Washingtonians alike find an excuse to stroll the grounds along the Tidal Basin. The trees only sometimes oblige planners by timing their splendor to coincide with the city's famous Cherry Blossom Festival. ABOVE: Thomas Jefferson himself introduced the classical colonnade style into the new United States. So architect John Russell Pope borrowed the design for the memorial to Jefferson. Its walls are inscribed with some of Jefferson's writings. OVERLEAF: As seen from the tiny observation area of the Washington Monument, the Potomac River snakes past the Jefferson Memorial and National Airport on its way to the Chesapeake Bay. Not just autos but also Washington's sleek Metrorail transit cars whiz over the river to Alexandria and the airport.

The rear of the White House, facing the Ellipse and less visible to the public than the 1600 Pennsylvania Avenue address around front, includes the Rose Garden, the windows of the elliptical Oval Office, and Harry Truman's second-story porch. Marine One, *the president's helicopter, lands on the South Lawn.* OPPOSITE: *A fresh snowfall coats the* lawn in front of the 132-room Executive Mansion. The president is rarely seen here, except to greet visiting dignitaries, though the family dining room—off limits to visitors—faces Pennsylvania Avenue. Concerns about the First Family's safety prompted the Secret Service to close this stretch of the avenue to vehicular traffic in 1995.

Alfred B. Mullett's Old Executive Office Building—the ornate, French Empire warren of offices for the president's staff—was detested when it was completed in 1888. When President William Howard Taft later named a Fine Arts Commission to plan new executive department buildings, Commissioner Cass Gilbert told a friend he hoped each chosen architect would be anything but "a cubist, a futurist, or a Mullett." Today, the chaotic building is much loved. ABOVE: Robert Mills, designer of the Washington Monument, also planned the enormous Treasury Building. Some say that President Jackson ordered it plunked where it is— blocking the vista to the Capitol—in a fit of pique against Congress. Truth was, Congress itself chose the site because it lay on cheap government land.

The Capitol reflecting pool, added to the grounds in 1971, is presided over by a statue of Ulysses S. Grant. It offers a serene interlude between the frenzy inside the legislative chambers and the vigorous tenor of Independence, Constitution, and Pennsylvania avenues to the west. ABOVE: The Peace Monument, built in 1877, honors the U.S. Navy's Civil War dead. OVERLEAF: Constantino Brumidi's 1865 fresco, Apotheosis, is constructed in two rings—the inner representing the thirteen original states of the Union, and the outer depicting four hundred years of American history.

Only the Library of Congress's most esteemed researchers have access to the Members' Room, whose ornamentation includes a marble fireplace topped by Frederick Dielman's mosaic depicting History with Mythology and Tradition. America's oldest national cultural institution was opened in 1800 inside the U.S. Capitol. When most of its collection was destroyed by British torches in 1814, Thomas Jefferson sold to Congress (for $23,950) 6,487 of his personal works, in several languages. The collection has grown to well over one hundred million items, four-fifths in formats other than books.

OPPOSITE: The lavish Great Hall of the Jefferson Building was restored to mark the building's centennial in 1997. This sculpture by Philip Martiny stands at the foot of the Great Staircase. OVERLEAF: In the days when dozens of steam locomotives chugged past the Library's open windows on their way to Union Station, soot turned the Jefferson Building's magnificent artwork a dingy yellow, then almost black.

The aura of the United States Supreme Court Building is imposing, but it is among Washington's twenty top tourist sites. When the High Court convenes, visitors may hear a sample of lawyers' and justices' arguments in a brief walkthrough. Or they may arrive early in hopes of securing one of the few seats available to the public for the entire day. Architect Cass Gilbert designed this legal temple after William Howard Taft, the only president to also serve as chief justice, pushed to get the justices a courthouse of their own.

A block of shops and small office buildings was razed to build the hulking $126-million FBI Building, which was immediately panned by architectural critics. One termed it "the Nightmare on Pennsylvania Avenue." The bureau's security-conscious director, J. Edgar Hoover—who himself called it ugly—permitted few entrances into his fortress, and street vendors were forbidden from setting up beneath it. LEFT: Michael Lantz's statue Man Controlling Trade sits outside the Federal Trade Commission Building at the apex of the Federal Triangle. Construction of the wall of the uniformly designed limestone buildings between the Mall and Pennsylvania Avenue was the largest public building project in American history.

ARCHIVES OF THE UNITED STATES OF AMERICA

When John F. Kennedy rode up Pennsylvania Avenue in his inaugural parade, he was aghast at its tackiness. "It's a disgrace," he is reported to have said. "Fix it." One of the results of a thirty-year makeover is tranquil Pershing Park (left), which is full of grasses, water lilies, and even lotuses in its pond. OPPOSITE: John Russell Pope designed the imposing National Archives Building more than a decade before he worked on the Jefferson Memorial. ABOVE: Robert Aitken's allegorical sculpture What Is Past Is Prologue greets Archives Building visitors.

Dry-goods dealers, tanners, several undertakers' offices, and two woolen mills once filled Market Square, across Pennsylvania Avenue from busy Center Market. As part of Pennsylvania Avenue's rebirth, Market Square came alive with twin neo-classical towers. Two separate projects included upscale housing units and restaurants that added energy and nightlife to the city's long-dormant main street.

ABOVE: The modest Navy Memorial fills Market Square's courtyard. A simple bronze Lone Sailor statue stands on a giant stone disk inscribed with a world map.

OVERLEAF: About 250,000 people, including veterans of all the nation's wars, are buried at Arlington National Cemetery, where an average of eighteen funerals are held each day.

Maya Ying Lin, a Yale University architecture student, designed "The Wall" at the Vietnam Veterans Memorial (above). Friends and loved ones often make tracings from the more than 58,000 names etched into the wall. Or they leave poignant souvenirs, some of which are displayed at the Smithsonian Institu- tion's National Museum of American History. LEFT: Eleven years after the completion of the Vietnam Veterans Memorial, a Vietnam Women's Memorial (© 1993, V.W.M.P., Inc.; Glenna Good- acre, sculptor) was added nearby. It depicts two uni- formed women caring for a wounded male soldier.

In 1995, the Korean War Veterans Memorial (© KWVM Productions, Inc.) was unveiled across the Mall reflecting pool from the Vietnam Veterans Memorial. Highlighting the timeless theme "Freedom Is Not Free," the memorial was designed by Washington's Cooper•Lecky Architects. It depicts nineteen battle-clad, stainless-steel troopers, created by Frank Gaylord, warily venturing into the open and heading for a giant American flag. To their side is a black granite wall, designed by Louis Nelson Associates, into which are etched the faces of more than twenty-five hundred support troops, taken from photographs. ABOVE: Each trooper wears a heavy poncho—standard issue for Korea's heavy rains and bitter cold.

Robert Berks's memorial to Albert Einstein stands outside the National Research Council building. The granite figure holds a tablet showing three of his important equations, including one that summarizes the theory of general relativity. BOTTOM: The statue of Mary McLeod Bethune rests opposite an emancipation monument in Lincoln Park off East Capitol Street. Also executed by Robert Berks, it was commissioned by the National Council of Negro Women, which Bethune founded. OPPOSITE: A third Berks work, the bust of President John F. Kennedy, dominates the lobby of the Kennedy Center for the Performing Arts. Its six theaters present more musical and artistic performances than any other single institution in the nation. OVERLEAF: The Smithsonian's sandstone "Castle" building on the Washington Mall houses the visitor center for the vast scientific institution.

"Meet me at the elephant" is a familiar refrain among families who visit the museums on the Washington Mall. This beast is the centerpiece of the Smithsonian Institution's National Museum of Natural History. The remains of thousands more creatures help depict the history of the natural world and human cultures. ABOVE: One of the most enduringly popular Smithsonian exhibits is the array of First Ladies' formal gowns, displayed at the National Museum of American History, which also examines American artifacts as mundane as the bicycle and washing machine. OVERLEAF: Known for its rockets, space capsules, and thrilling IMAX movies, the Air and Space Museum also displays the most vintage of all aircraft, the Wright Brothers' Flyer.

One of the lesser-known Smithsonian galleries is the National Museum of American Art, removed from the Mall in the Gallery Place–Chinatown neighborhood across Pennsylvania Avenue. It features American paintings, sculpture, graphics, folk art, and photography of the eighteenth century to the present. BOTTOM: The Renwick Gallery is an offshoot of the National Museum of American Art. Also located some distance from the Mall, across the street from the White House, it displays American crafts. OPPOSITE: The Smithsonian's National Portrait Gallery shares the old Patent Office Building with the National Museum of American Art. When Robert Mills finished the huge quadrangular structure in 1867, it was the largest building in the country. The gallery displays the portraits of distinguished Americans like George Washington and features a Civil War exhibition.

The National Museum of African Art (above), behind the "Castle," is another Smithsonian gallery. It holds more than six thousand works of traditional art from sub-Saharan Africa. RIGHT: South African muralist Esther Mahlangu created a Ndebele wall painting on a façade of the annex of the National Museum of Women in the Arts, on New York Avenue. OPPOSITE: The United States Holocaust Memorial Museum displays disturbing reminders of a barbaric chapter in world history. But it also recalls more sanguine times in the lives of Holocaust victims. OVERLEAF: Columns removed from the U.S. Capitol form an imposing peristyle at the 444-acre United States National Arboretum, which includes the National Bonsai Collection and the National Herb Garden.

Work began on the Washington National Cathedral (left), the world's sixth-largest cathedral, in 1907 and took eighty-three years to complete. The Episcopal Church oversees the Gothic cathedral, but several denominations hold services there. OPPOSITE: The peal of bells from the National Shrine of the Immaculate Conception can be heard across the campus of the Catholic University of America and beyond. Every parish in the nation contributed to the construction of America's largest Catholic church. OVERLEAF: The illuminated tower of the Temple of the Church of Jesus Christ of Latter-Day Saints, topped by the statue of the Mormon angel Moroni, is a landmark along the Capital Beltway in suburban Maryland. Once, a brazen thief in a helicopter tried unsuccessfully to wrench the golden statue from its moorings.

The gardens of Mount Vernon, President Washington's Potomac River estate, are legendary. Washington was his own landscape architect. He often wrote home to instruct groundskeepers in the gardens' care. In his diary, he once noted, "Road to my Mill Swamp . . . in search of the sort of Trees I shall want for my Walks, groves and Wildernesses." ABOVE: The nucleus of the Mount Vernon mansion was constructed about 1735 by Washington's father, Augustine. Fourteen rooms, containing numerous original furnishings, are open for viewing. When the Mount Vernon Ladies' Association bought and saved the estate in 1858, it inspired the American preservation movement. The estate, south of Alexandria, Virginia, along a scenic parkway, is reachable by automobile, bus connection to the Metro subway, the Washington Tourmobile, and even by boat.

There is a National Historic Site in Washington's Anacostia neighborhood, marking the home of abolitionist Frederick Douglass. But he is remembered elsewhere as well, as in this Massachusetts Avenue mural. Douglass created the Freedman's Savings Bank during the Civil War for the use of black Union troops and former slaves. RIGHT: Sixteenth Street, leading uptown directly from the White House, was once the city's most fashionable address. It was the first Embassy Row before many nations built even more impressive mansions along Massachusetts Avenue. Even tattered by age and mistreatment, the magnificent brownstones farther up Sixteenth, Fourteenth, and Thirteenth streets recall a gentler age of gaslights and surreys.